WHY DO BEES HUM?
And 265 Other Great Jokes for Kids

WHY DO BEES HUM?* And 265 Other Great Jokes for Kids

By Gary Chmielewski
Drawings by Ron G. Clark

DERRYDALE BOOKS
New York • Avenel, New Jersey

This 1990 edition is published by Derrydale Books, distributed by Outlet Book Company, Inc.,
a Random House Company, 40 Engelhard Avenue, Avenel, New Jersey 07001,
by arrangement with Rourke Enterprises, Inc.

Random House
New York • Toronto • London • Sydney • Auckland

Manufactured in the United States of America

Library of Congress Cataloging-in-Publication Data
Chmielewski, Gary, 1946
    Why do bees hum? and 265 other great jokes for kids/by Gary Chmielewski.
       p.   cm.
    Originally published in 5 separate volumes: Riddles, Sports jokes, Teacher jokes, Knock-
knocks, and Animal jokes.
    ISBN 0-517-02536-1
    1. Wit and humor. Juvenile.   2. Riddles, Juvenile.   [1. Jokes. 2. Riddles.]   I. Title.
PN6163.C46   1990   818′.5402 – dc20   90-3182   CIP   AC

12   11   10   9   8   7   6

CONTENTS

ANIMAL JOKES

What animals do you find at every baseball game?
BATS!

What does a skunk do when it's angry?
It raises a stink!

A donkey seeing a zebra for the first time said to himself "Imagine that! A donkey that's been to jail!"

What do bees do with their honey?
They cell it.

What animal eats with its tail?
They all do. No animal removes its tail to eat!

Which dog always knows what time it is?
A watch dog!

What is cow hide used for?
To hold the cow together!

4

Jimmy: I went swimming today and a fish bit off one of my fingers.
Tommy: Which one?
Jimmy: I don't know. All fish look alike.

What did one fish say to the other fish after it was hooked?
"That's what you get for not keeping your mouth shut!"

What do dogs and trees have in common?
Their bark!

What did one firefly say to the other firefly?
Your son sure is bright for his age!

Jack: Your dog just bit my ankle.

Mary: What did you expect? He's just a small dog and can't reach any higher!

What fish goes well with peanut butter in your sandwich?
A jelly fish!

First Hunter: I just ran into a big bear!
Second Hunter: Did you let him have both barrels?
First Hunter: Both barrels — I let him have the whole gun!

What kind of cat hangs around a bowling alley?
An alley cat!

What kind of dog hands out tickets?
A police dog!

Why did the elephant quit the circus?
He didn't want to work for peanuts anymore!

Which fish go to heaven when they die?
Angel fish!

Why did the farmer put bells on his cows?
The horns didn't work!

Why are cats larger at night than in the day?
Because they're let out at night and taken in in the morning!

Did you hear the story about the peacock?
No.
Well, it's a beautiful tale!

What kind of dog can be found at a bowling alley?
A setter!

Gail: I got a cow for my birthday.
Tom: Does it give milk?
Gail: No, I have to take it from her.

What kind of sharks never eat women?
Man-eating sharks!

Why do ducks dive?
They want to liquidate their bills!

A young man was helping a farmer herd some cattle when the farmer asked him to hold the bull for a moment.
"No sir," said the young man. "I don't mind being a director in this operation, but I don't want to be a stockholder!"

Little Girl: How much are those puppies in the window?
Pet Store Owner: Twenty dollars a piece.
Little Girl: How much is a whole one?

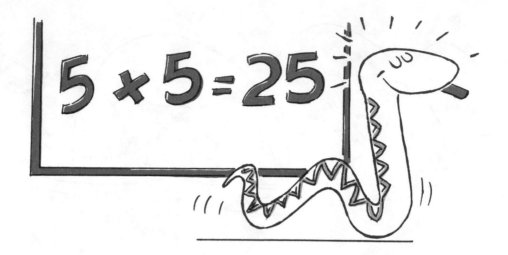

What kind of snake is very good at math?
An adder.

Crockett: I've got an alligator on my boat named Ginger.
Tubbs: Does Ginger bite?
Crockett: No, Ginger snaps!

Bobby: I've got a cat who can say his own name.
Charlie: That's great! What's your cat's name?
Bobby: "Meow"!

Julie: My dog Chewbacca is sick, so we're taking him to an animal doctor.

Stevie: Gee, I thought all doctors were people.

17

What should you do when a bull charges you?
Pay him!

Charles: My parents bought me a bird for my birthday.
Rita: What kind?
Charles: A keet.
Rita: You mean a parakeet.
Charles: No, they only bought me one!

What did the baby chicken say when it saw an orange in the mother's nest?
Look at the orange Mama laid!

Veterinarian: Has your dog ever had fleas?
Little Boy: No, only puppies!

Belinda: We have a new dog.
George: What's he like?
Belinda: Anything we feed him!

Nancy: How do you get down off an elephant?

Robert: You climb down.

Nancy: WRONG!

Robert: You grease his sides and slide down.

Nancy: WRONG!

Robert: You get a ladder and climb down.

Nancy: WRONG! You can't get down off an elephant. You get it off a goose!

What did the man say when his dog ran away?
Doggone-it!

Mother tiger to baby tiger: What are you doing?

Baby tiger: I'm chasing a hunter around the tree.

Mother tiger: How often do I have to tell you not to play with your food!

What' a fighter's favorite dog?
A boxer!

What kind of snake snaps at people?
A garter snake!

What do you call a cat who drinks lemonade?
A sour puss!

How many legs does a mule have if you call a tail a leg?
Four — calling a tail a leg doesn't make it a leg.

What did the elephant say when he sat on the box of cookies?
That's the way the cookies crumble!

What is a boxer's favorite bird?
A duck!

SPORTS JOKES

When is a boxer like an astronomer?
When he sees stars!

George: What's the score of the game?
Belinda: 21 to 13
George: Who's winning?
Belinda: 21

Why would a spider make a good outfielder?
He's good at catching flies!

Arnie: I always carry a spare pair of pants with me when I golf.
Sammy: Why?
Arnie: I might get a hole-in-one.

What three "R's" do cheerleaders have to learn?
Rah! Rah! Rah!

What two things can't a runner have for breakfast?
Lunch and dinner!

Rookie: How do you hold a bat?
Veteran: By its wings.

Why is bowling such a quiet game?
You can hear a pin drop!

Where do judges go to relax?
The tennis court!

Why is the stadium the coolest place?
All the fans are in the stands.

Why did the basketball player bring a shotgun to the game?
He wanted to shoot the ball!

Reporter: Have you ever hunted bear?
Sportsman: No, but I've gone fishing in my bathing suit!

Did you hear about the person who went to the football game because he thought the quarterback was a refund?

What kind of sand would you run in if you wanted to be faster?
Quicksand!

Does horseback riding give you a headache?
No, quite the reverse!

Paul: Doctor, will I be able to play soccer after my leg heals?
Doctor: Of course.
Paul: Great. I never could play before.

What monster goes to baseball games?
A double-header!

Henry: Did you hear the new song about baseball?
Babe: No, why?
Henry: You should, it's a really big hit!

Julie: I don't play tennis anymore because it's too noisy.
Debbie: Too noisy?
Julie: Yeah, everyone raises a racket.

Why is a basketball player's hand never larger than eleven inches?
If it were twelve inches, it would be a foot!

Which professional football team has the largest players?
The New York GIANTS!

To what football game do you have to bring crackers and a spoon?
The Soup-er Bowl! (Yeah – Chicago Bears)

Rookie: What does it take to hit a ball the way you do?
Veteran: A bat.

Little Girl: What kind of fish is that?
Fisherman: Smelt.
Little Girl: It sure does. But what kind of fish is it?

Umpire: I have to admit, the players on your team are good losers.
Coach: Good? They're perfect!

Christy: We can't go swimming right now. After eating, mom said we shouldn't swim on a full stomach.

Laura: Okay – we'll swim on our backs.

Game Warden: Kids, you can't fish without a permit!

Jimmy: Not so, sir. We're using worms and the fish are biting like crazy!

Basketball fan: I bet I can tell you the score of this game before it starts.

Sportcaster: Okay, smartie, tell me.

Basketball fan: Nothing to nothing.

What has 18 legs and catches flies?
A baseball team.

Why should everyone run?
We all belong to the human race!

In what part of the car do you keep your baseball mitt?
The glove compartment!

Why is it so hard to drive a golf ball?
No steering wheel!

Did you hear about the college athlete who won a letter in football
and asked a friend to read it to him?

First Hunter: This must be a good place for hunting.
Second Hunter: How do you know?
First Hunter: The sign said "Fine For Hunting!"

Charles: I went riding today.
Diana: Horseback?
Charles: Sure — about two hours before me.

Gary: My father went hunting today and shot three turkeys.
Laura: Were they wild?
Gary: No, but the farmer who owned them sure was.

Baseball Manager to Outfielders: You've been missing a lot of balls out there lately. If you can't do any better, I'm going to have to put in some other players.
Outfielders: Gee thanks! We can use the help!

What do eggs and a losing ball team have in common?
They both get beaten.

Jean: I've been skiing since I was five years old.
Ron: You must really be tired!

Who won at Bull Run?
I don't know — was the score in the papers?

What's a mosquito's favorite sport?
Skin diving!

How do you kiss a hockey player?
You pucker up!

Why was the baseball player arrested after the season?
He stole 85 bases.

Gary: Why don't you play golf with Terry anymore?
Jimmy: Would you play with a cheat who moves the ball when you're not looking and writes down the wrong score?
Gary: Certainly not!
Jimmy: Well, neither will Terry!

Why are waiters and waitresses such good tennis players?
They know how to serve!

Which football player wears the biggest shoes?
The one with the biggest feet.

Why is basketball such a sloppy sport?
All the players dribble!

Why is an airline pilot like a running back?
They both want to make a touchdown!

Old Fisherman: Did you ever take home a fish this size, sonny?
Sonny: No, sir. I always throw the little ones back.

Why does it take longer to run from second base to third than it does from first to second base?
There's a shortstop between second and third.

Game Warden: Do you know that you are hunting with last year's license?
Hunter: It's okay – I'm only after the ones that got away last year!

What do a bat and a fly swatter have in common?
They both hit flies.

Game Warden: Young man, there's no fishing here!
Young Man: You're telling me! I've been here for two hours and haven't had a bite.

Charlie: Mom, I'm going out to play soccer.
Mom: With your new slacks?
Charlie: No, with the boys down the street!

Why couldn't the fans drink soda during the second baseball game?
The home team lost the opener.

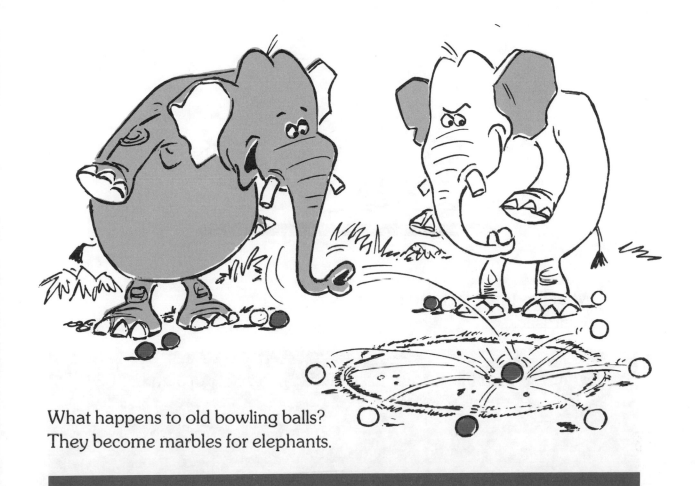

What happens to old bowling balls?
They become marbles for elephants.

Gail: I'm taking a course in parachute jumping.
Tommy: How many jumps do you have to make before you pass the course?
Gail: All of them!

What has three feet and no legs?
A yardstick.

What was the chicken farmer doing at the basketball game?
Looking for fouls (fowls)!

Which winter sport do you learn in the fall?
Ice skating!

What's the biggest jewel in the world?
A baseball diamond.

TEACHER JOKES

Teacher to Student: Why would you bring your duck with you to class?

Student: I want him to be a wise quacker.

English Teacher: "What is an autobiography?"
Ron: "I know! I know! It's the life story of a car!"

Math Teacher: "If I cut a steak into two parts, what would I get?"
Gail: "Halves."
Teacher: "Right, and then cut in half again?"
Gail: "Quarters."
Teacher: "And again?"
Gail: "Eighths."
Teacher: "And again?"
Gail: "Hamburgers!"

What did Pat do when her puppy chewed up her dictionary?
She took the words right out of his mouth.

Rita: "Mom, I learned to write in school today."
Mother: "What did you write?"
Rita: "I don't know, I haven't learned to read yet!"

Teacher: "Did your mother help you with your homework?"
Tanya: "No."
Teacher: "Are you sure?"
Tanya: "Yes, she didn't help me – she did it all!"

Math Teacher: "If you put your hand in your right pocket and found 75¢, and then put your hand in your left pocket and found 50¢, what would you have?"
George: "Someone else's pants!"

Mother: "Julie, why are you crying?"
Julie: "My teacher yelled at me for something I didn't do."
Mother: "What was it you didn't do?"
Julie: "My homework!"

What animal runs around the classroom stealing answers?
A Cheetah.

What is a warlock's favorite subject?
Spelling!

Why did the teacher date the new custodian?
He swept her off her feet.

How do you like school?
Closed!

Student: "Is it true that the law of gravity keeps us on this earth?"
Teacher: "Yes."
Student: "What did we do before the law was passed?"

Teacher: "What's the matter, Tommy?"
Tommy: "I don't want to scare you, but my mother said if I didn't get better grades, someone is going to get punished!"

"Mother, could you help me with my homework?"
"It wouldn't be right."
"I know – but you could at least try!"

Teacher: "Why are you running?"
Boy: "I'm running to stop a fight."
Teacher: "Between who?"
Boy: "Me and the guy who's chasing me!"

Teacher: "Laura, I hope I didn't see you looking over at Christy's test."

Laura: "I hope so too."

Were the test questions hard?
No, the questions were easy. It was the answers that were hard!

What marks did you get in physical education last year?
I didn't get any marks, only bruises!

What's a snake's favorite subject?
Hiss-tory.

Billy's Mother: "Billy told me he got 100 on his tests yesterday."
Counselor: "He did. A 50 in spelling and a 50 in arithmetic."

Teacher: "This is the fifth time this week I've had to punish you. What do you have to say for yourself?"
Chuck: "Thank goodness it's Friday!"

Father: "What does this 'F' on your report card mean?"
Son: "Fantastic!"

When should teachers wear sunglasses?
When they have bright students.

Teacher: "A, B, C, D, E, F, G. What comes after G?"
Gary: "Whiz!"

Teacher: "Tom, you've been late to school every day since school began. What's the reason?"

Tom: "I can't help it. The sign on the street says, 'School. Go Slow'."

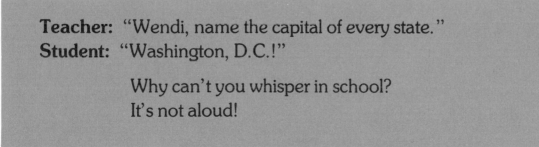

Teacher: "Wendi, name the capital of every state."
Student: "Washington, D.C.!"

Why can't you whisper in school?
It's not aloud!

Where is your homework paper?
You won't believe this, but I made a paper airplane out of it and
someone hijacked it!

Teacher: "Well, there's one good thing I can say about your son."
Father: "Oh? What's that?"
Teacher: "With grades like his, he can't possibly be cheating!"

Counselor: "How are your marks in school?"
Student: "Under water."
Counselor: "What do you mean?"
Student: "Below C-level!"

Mother: "I know my daughter talks a lot in class, but she is trying."
Teacher: "She sure is!"

Student: "I don't think I deserve a zero on this test."
Teacher: "Neither do I, but it's the lowest grade I can give you!"

English Teacher: "John, your spelling is terrible. Don't you ever read a dictionary?"
John: "No, I'll wait for the movie!"

Chemistry Teacher: "What is the formula for vanishing?"
Pupils: "Hey bub a ree bub!"
Teacher: "That's right! Oh my!"

Where is the English Channel?
I don't know, our television set doesn't pick it up!

Why do students have such good eyesight?
They're pupils.

Teacher: "Children, open your geography books. Who can tell me where Mexico is?"
Laura: "I know — I know. It's on page 31!"

What three words do teachers like most about their jobs?
June, July, and August.

"Teacher, I can't do this problem."
"Any six-year-old should be able to do it."
"Well, no wonder I can't. I'm ten."

Daughter: "Dad, can you write your name in the dark?"
Dad: "I think so."
Daughter: "Great. Would you please turn off the lights and sign my report card?"

English Teacher: "Who was Homer?"
Bobbie: "Didn't he invent baseball?"

Science Teacher: "Who can tell me what an atom is?"
Student: "Isn't that the guy who went out with Eve?"

Why did Charlie bake his term paper?
The teacher said he wanted it well done.

"Class, you've all been very noisy, so you'll all have to stay after school."
"Give me liberty or give me death."
"Who said that?"
"Patrick Henry!"

Science Teacher: "What is a comet?"
Student: "I don't know."
Teacher: "Don't you know what they call a star with a tail?"
Student: "Oh, sure. Lassie."

Parents: "Everything is going up – the price of food, clothing, everything. I wish something would go down."

Daughter: "Take a look at my report card!"

Why do you hate school?
I don't hate school, it's the principal of the thing!

What did one math book say to another math book?
Boy, do I have problems.

Principal: "Why are you late this morning?"
Student: "Because of the alarm clock. Everyone got up except for me."
Principal: "How was that?"
Student: "There are eight of us in the family and the alarm was set for seven!"

RIDDLES

How do you make an egg roll?
Push it down the hill.

Why is electricity so dangerous?
It doesn't know how to conduct itself.

Why was the wheel such an important invention?
It got everything else going.

What is the deepest part of the Pacific Ocean?
The bottom.

What kind of umbrella does Superman carry on a rainy day?
A wet one.

Why is an old car like a baby?
They both have a rattle.

What bird is at your meal?
A swallow.

Three fat men were walking under one small umbrella, but none got wet. Why?
It wasn't raining.

When is it proper to serve milk in a saucer?
When you feed a cat.

What did the mayonnaise say to the refrigerator?
"Close the door. Can't you see I'm dressing?"

Why did Christy go outside with her purse open?
She heard there would be some change in the weather.

When is a mystery writer like a vegetable farmer?
When he digs up a plot.

Why should potatoes act better than other vegetables?
They have eyes to see what they are doing.

What did the corn stalk say to the farmer?
"Stop picking on me!"

Where do children grow?
In a kindergarten.

Why are flowers lazy?
Because you always find them in beds.

What time is it when a clock strikes 13?
Time to get it fixed.

When can you carry water in a strainer?
When it is frozen.

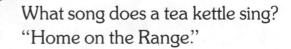

What song does a tea kettle sing?
"Home on the Range."

What are the smartest animals in the sea?
Fish. They go around in schools.

Why did the mother knit three socks for her son?
He grew another foot over the winter.

When do one and one not make two?
When they make 11.

When the apple wanted to fight the banana, why did the banana run away?
Because it was yellow.

Some months have thirty days. Some months have thirty-one days. How many months have twenty-eight days?
All of them.

Why do bees hum?
Because they don't know the words.

What did the big firecracker say to the little firecracker?
"My pop is bigger than your pop!"

If you lived in a cemetery, with what would you open the gate?
A skeleton key.

What is the tallest building in your city?
The library – it has the most stories.

How do monsters count to fifteen?
They use their fingers.

What did the ocean say when the plane flew over?
Nothing – it just waved.

How is a book like a tree?
They both have leaves.

What country can't get enough to eat?
Hungary.

What country helps you to cook?
Greece.

How do you know an elephant will stay for a long time when it comes to visit?
It brings its trunk.

Why is Santa Claus like the Farmer-in-the-Dell?
They both like to hoe, hoe, hoe.

Why did Robin Hood only steal from the rich to give to the poor?
It wouldn't have worked the other way.

Why does an Indian wear feathers?
To keep his wigwarm/'wig warm'.

What is black and white and has sixteen wheels?
A zebra on roller skates.

Why does a spider make a good baseball player?
Because it catches flies.

Why did the boy put on a wet shirt and pants?
The label said "wash and wear".

Where was the Magna Carta signed?
At the bottom.

In what battle did General Wolfe cry, "I die happy"?
His last one!

What kind of dog does a person bite?
A hot dog!

Why did the fireman wear red suspenders?
To keep his pants up.
Why did the fireman wear blue suspenders?
Because he couldn't find his red ones.

Why does a dog wag its tail?
Because no one else will wag it for him.

Which moves faster — hot or cold?
Hot. Anybody can catch a cold.

What tree can you carry in your hand?
Palm.

What kind of candy bar can you find in outer space?
Milky Way.

How many hamburgers can you eat on an empty stomach?
One. After that your stomach is no longer empty.

Why is a rabbit's nose always so shiny?
Because its powder puff is on the wrong end.

What goes all the way from New York to Chicago without moving?
Railroad tracks.

Why is watermelon filled with water?
It's planted in the spring.

Why did the worker sit on a clock?
He wanted to work overtime.

What did the rug say to the floor?
"Don't move. I have you covered!"

Why did the boy throw the clock off the roof?
He wanted to see time fly.

How much dirt can you take out of a hole three feet, three feet by two feet?
None. The dirt has already been taken out.

What are the largest ants in the world?
Gi-ants.

How much water can you put in an empty glass?
None. It wouldn't be empty.

If a king sits on gold, who sits on silver?
The Lone Ranger.

KNOCK KNOCKS

Knock, Knock
Who's there?
Morris
Morris who?
Morris in the pot, so help yourself.

Knock, Knock
Who's there?
Olive
Olive who?
Olive a parade!

Knock, Knock
Who's there
Celia
Celia who?
Celia later, alligator.

Knock, Knock
Who's there?
Howie
Howie who?
Howie doing with these Knock-Knock Jokes?

Knock, Knock
Who's there?
Myra
Myra who?
Myra frigerator needs defrosting.

Knock, Knock
Who's there?
Wanda
Wanda who?
Wanda have a little fun tonight?

100

Knock, Knock
Who's there?
Letter
Letter who?
Letter in. It's cold outside!

Knock, Knock
Who's there?
Knecklace
Knecklace who?
Knecklace people don't get sore throats.

Knock, Knock
Who's there?
Jose
Jose who?
"Jose can you see by the dawn's early light?"

Knock, Knock
Who's there?
Cargo
Cargo who?
Cargo beep-beep!

Knock, Knock
Who's there?
Freeze
Freeze who?
Freeze a jolly good fellow.

Knock, Knock
Who's there?
Amos
Amos who?
A mosquito bit me.

Knock, Knock
Who's there?
Andy
Andy who?
And he bit me again.

Knock, Knock
Who's there?
Esther
Esther who?
Esther a bug in your soup?

Knock, Knock
Who's there?
Hair
Hair who?
Hair today, gone tomorrow.

Knock, Knock
Who's there?
Cantaloupe
Cantaloupe who?
Cantaloupe, I'm already married.

Knock, Knock
Who's there?
Atch
Atch who?
Gesundheit!

Knock, Knock
Who's there?
Avocado
Avocado who?
Avocado cold!

Knock, Knock
Who's there?
Alma
Alma who?
Alma cookies are gone,
    and I want some more!

Knock, Knock
Who's there?
Dog
Dog who?
Doggone it, open the door.
It's snowing out here!

Knock, Knock
Who's there?
Isabel
Isabel who?
Isabel on your bike?

Knock, Knock
Who's there?
Ferd
Ferd who?
Ferd any good Knock-Knocks lately?

Knock, Knock
Who's there?
Seth
Seth who?
Seth me – And what I seth, goes.

Knock, Knock
Who's there?
O'Shea
O'Shea who?
O'Shea can you shee,
    by the dawn's early light.

Knock, Knock
Who's there?
Leaf
Leaf who?
Please, leaf me alone.

Knock, Knock
Who's there?
Canada
Canada who?
Canada dog come ina da house?

Knock, Knock
Who's there?
Phillip
Phillip who?
Phillip my tank, please.

Knock, Knock
Who's there?
Debris
Debris who?
Debris or not debris, dat is the question.

Knock, Knock
Who's there?
Denny
Denny who?
I don't know. Denny he tell you his name?

111

Knock, Knock
Who's there?
Gopher
Gopher who?
Gopher a touchdown, rah rah.

Knock, Knock
Who's there?
Hugo
Hugo who?
Hugo your way and I'll go mine.

Knock, Knock
Who's there?
Otis
Otis who?
Otis a wonderful day
        for a ride in the park.

Knock, Knock
Who's there?
Howard
Howard who?
Howard is the ground when you slip on a banana peel.

Knock, Knock
Who's there?
Diesel
Diesel who?
Diesel be your last chance.

Knock, Knock
Who's there?
Ida
Ida who?
If Ida known you were coming,
        Ida baked a cake.

Knock, Knock
Who's there?
Fiddlestick
Fiddlestick who?
If your sneakers get holes,
    your fiddlestick out.

Knock, Knock
Who's there?
Banana
Knock, Knock
Who's there?
Banana.
Knock, Knock
Who's there?
Orange
Orange who?
Orange you glad I didn't
    say Banana?

Knock, Knock
Who's there?
Wayne
Wayne who?
Waynedrops keep
faw-wing on my head.

115

Knock, Knock
Who's there?
Chesterfield
Chesterfield who?
Chesterfield my leg so I slapped him.

Knock, Knock
Who's there?
Pizza
Pizza who?
Pizza on earth,
          good will to men.

Knock, Knock
Who's there?
Beets
Beets who?
Beets me; I forgot my name.

Knock, Knock
Who's there?
Reed
Reed who?
Reed this book and find out.

Knock, Knock
Who's there?
Freddy
Freddy who?
Freddy or not, here I come.

Knock, Knock
Who's there?
Utah
Utah who?
Utah a putty cat!

Knock, Knock
Who's there?
Victor
Victor who?
Victor his hair out!

Knock, Knock
Who's there?
Rhoda
Rhoda who?
Rhoda horse all the way through Texas.

Knock, Knock
Who's there?
Tuba
Tuba who?
Tuba toothpaste,

Knock, Knock
Who's there?
Shelby
Shelby who?
Shelby comin' round the mountain when she comes . . .

OO-HOO HOO HOO

Knock, Knock
Who's there?
Butter
Butter who?
Butter late than never.

Knock, Knock
Who's there?
Little old lady
Little old lady who?
Oh, I didn't know you could yodel!

120